THIS
prayer
JOURNAL

belongs to:

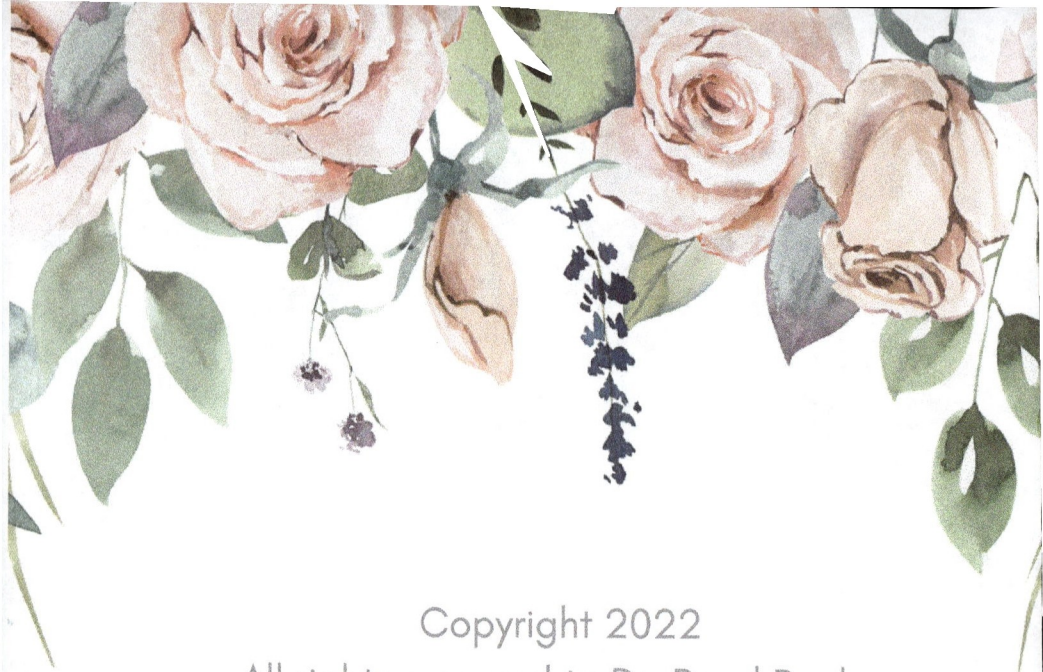

Hey There! Thank You for deciding to heal on purpose. Thank You for Trusting God with EVERY aspect of your life. Thank You for LIVING! Thank You for Trusting the God in Me to walk with you on this journey. I know it's not easy but YOU are worth it. IT IS WELL! This is Your Season, Walk in it! Live Out Loud and Love On Purpose. Trust God through the Process and You Will Win.
Love You On Purpose,
Dr. Pearl Pugh

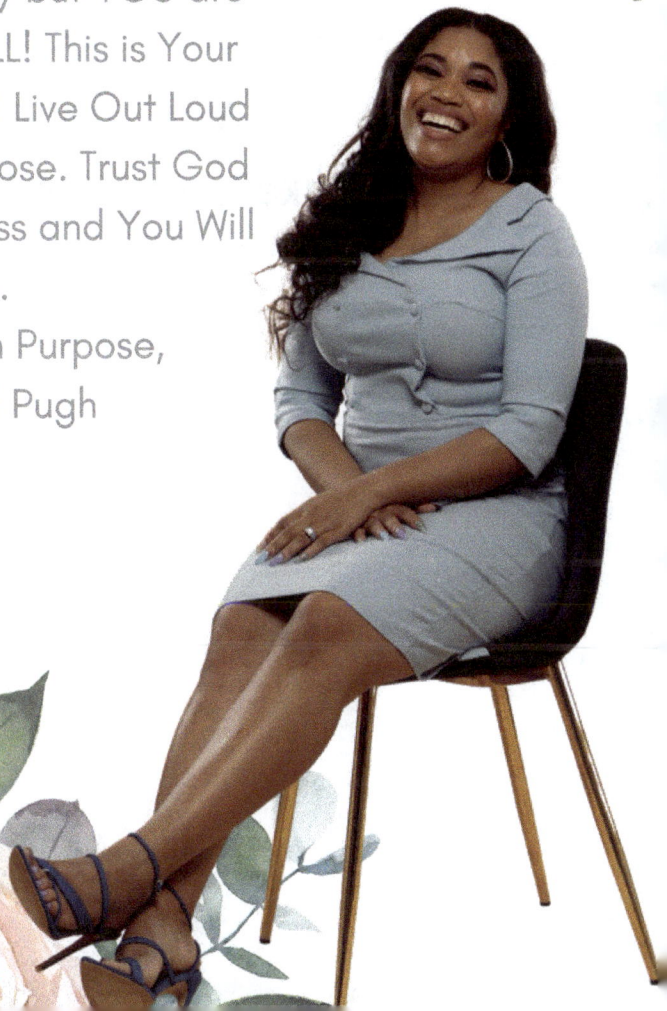

But when you ask, you must believe and
not doubt, because the one
who doubts is
like a wave of the sea,
blown and tossed
by the wind

James 1:6

Dear God,

_____
_____
_____
_____
_____
_____
_____
_____
_____
_____
_____
_____
_____
_____
_____
_____
_____
_____
_____
_____
_____
_____
........Amen
_____

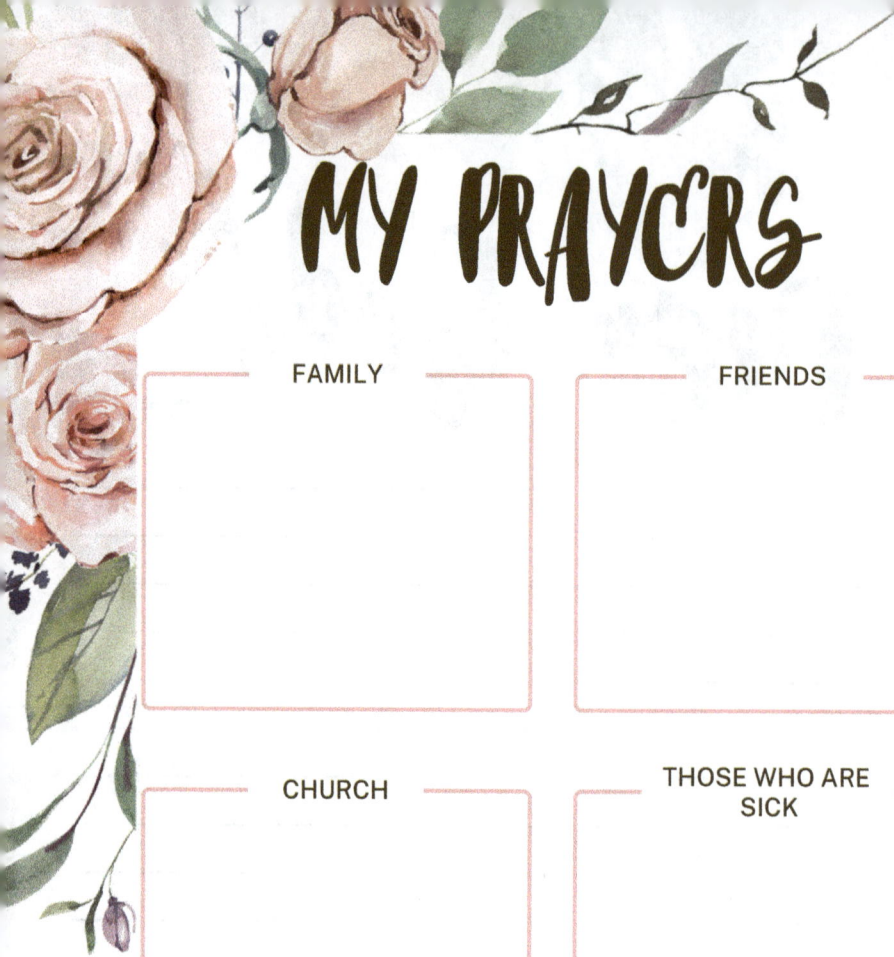

MY PRAYERS

FAMILY

FRIENDS

CHURCH

THOSE WHO ARE SICK

MYSELF

Verse of the DAy:

Gratitude

Reflection

Specific Prayer

I pray for:

_____
_____
_____
_____
_____
_____
_____
_____
_____
_____

Thank You Jesus

Scriptures:

☑   ☑

Father, help me not to lean on my own understanding, but in Everything acknowledge You. So that You can direct my words, thoughts and actions.

In Jesus' Mighty Name, Amen

I'm thankful for:

Inspirational Scripture.....

-
-
-
-

Lord help me.....

Reflection

And we know that in all things God works for the good of those who love him, who have been called according to his purpose. Romans 8:28

Prayers

I do believe;
help me
overcome
my unbelief!

Mark 9:24

Dear God,

_____
_____
_____
_____
_____
_____
_____
_____
_____
_____
_____
_____
_____
_____
_____
_____
_____
_____
_____
_____
.......Amen
_____

MY PRAYERS

FAMILY

FRIENDS

CHURCH

THOSE WHO ARE SICK

MYSELF

Verse of the DAy:

Gratitude

Reflection

Specific Prayer

I pray for:

_____
_____
_____
_____
_____
_____
_____
_____
_____

Thank You Jesus

Scriptures:

☑   ☑

Father in the name of Jesus, thank You for Your consistent love for me, Your blessings, and goodness. Thank You for Your faithfulness in guiding me and seeing me through uncertain times. Thank You for Your daily reminders of your promises and plans over my life. Thank You for never failing and always providing. Thank You for helping me walk boldly in every aspect of my life, knowing that all of my help comes from you. Please help me be a good steward and to sow wisely.

In Jesus' Mighty Name, Amen

I'm thankful for:

Inspirational Scripture.....

Lord help me.....

Reflection

The Lord is
far from the
wicked, but
he hears
the prayer
of the
righteous.

Proverbs 15:29

Prayers

Therefore if you have any encouragement from being united with Christ, if any comfort from His love, if any common sharing in the Spirit, if any tenderness and compassion, then make my joy complete by being like-minded, having the same love, being one in spirit and of one mind. Do nothing out of selfish ambition or vain conceit. Rather, in humility value others above yourselves, not looking to your own interests but each of you to the interests of the others.

Philippians 2:1-4

Dear God,

_____

_____

_____

_____

_____

_____

_____

_____

_____

_____

_____

_____

_____

_____

_____

_____

_____

_____

_____

_____

_____

_____

_____

........Amen

_____

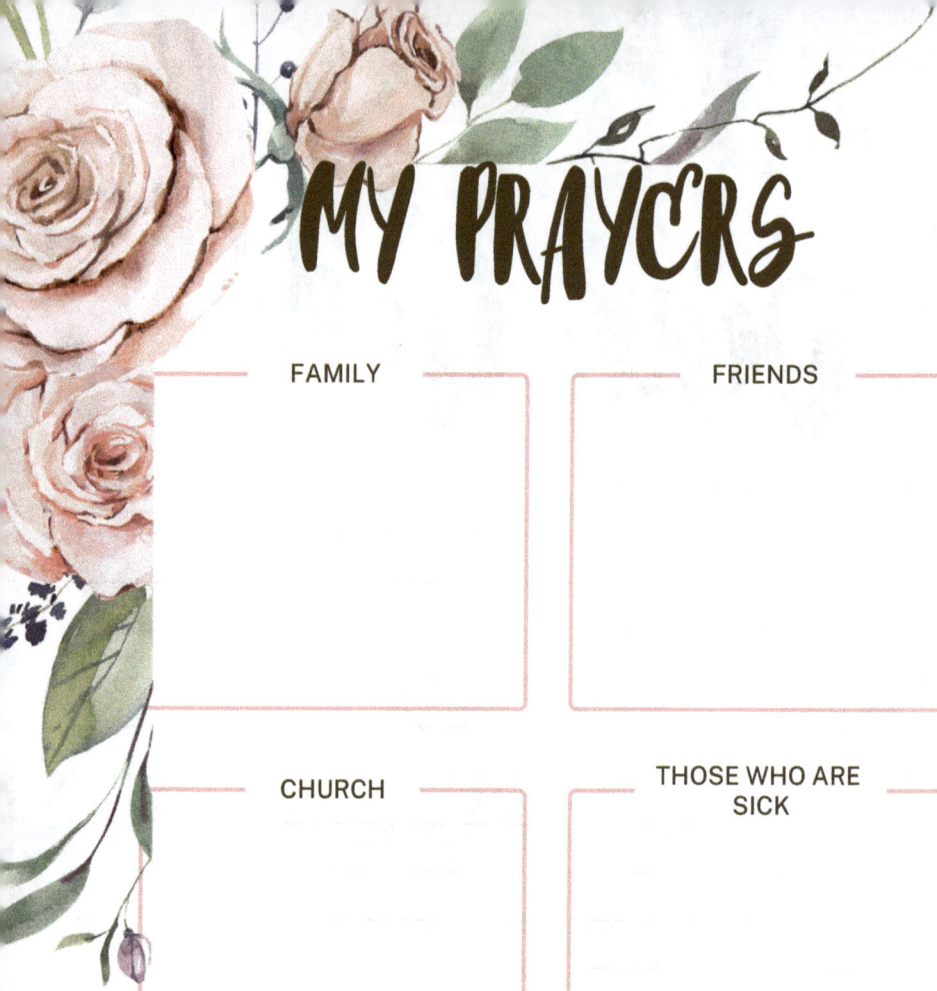

MY PRAYERS

FAMILY

FRIENDS

CHURCH

THOSE WHO ARE SICK

MYSELF

Verse of the DAy:

Gratitude

Reflection

Specific Prayer

I pray for:

_____
_____
_____
_____
_____
_____
_____
_____
_____

Scriptures:

☑   ☑

Thank You Jesus

Lord, thank you for being God to me. Thank you for making me strong in my weakest moments. Lord, please remove EVERYTHING that is not of you. Lord please give me EVERYTHING you desire for me to have. Father I bind anything that will keep me from having my focus on you. Give me a measure of your strength so that I might not give into discouragement, deception and doubt! Help me honor You in all my ways.

In Jesus' Mighty Name, Amen

I'm thankful for:

Inspirational Scripture.....

-
-
-
-

Lord help me.....

Reflection

When God saw what they did and how they turned from their evil ways, he relented and did not bring on them the destruction he had threatened.

Jonah 3:10

Prayers

But when you ask, you must believe and
not doubt, because the one
who doubts is
like a wave of the sea,
blown and tossed
by the wind

James 1:6

Dear God,

_____
_____
_____
_____
_____
_____
_____
_____
_____
_____
_____
_____
_____
_____
_____
_____
_____
_____
_____
_____
_____
........Amen
_____

MY PRAYERS

FAMILY

FRIENDS

CHURCH

THOSE WHO ARE SICK

MYSELF

Verse of the Day:

Gratitude

Reflection

Specific Prayer

I pray for:

_____

_____

_____

_____

_____

_____

_____

_____

_____

Scriptures:

☑   ☑

Thank You Jesus

Dear Lord, help me – every single day – to find faith in the midst of the chaos. Give me the desire and ability to understand You, receive You, talk to You, and give thanks to You. I pray that I will draw nearer and nearer to You, and that my faith will multiply exponentially.
In Jesus' Mighty Name, Amen

I'm thankful for:

spirational Scripture.....

Lord help me.....

Reflection

Do not wear yourself out to get rich; do not trust your own cleverness. Cast but a glance at riches, and they are gone, for they will surely sprout wings and fly off to the sky like an eagle.

Proverbs 23:4-5

Prayers

Whoever loves discipline loves knowledge, but whoever hates correction is stupid. Good people obtain favor from the Lord, but he condemns those who devise wicked schemes. No one can be established through wickedness, but the righteous cannot be uprooted. A wife of noble character is her husband's crown, but a disgraceful wife is like decay in his bones. The plans of the righteous are just, but the advice of the wicked is deceitful

Proverbs 12:1-5

Dear God,

_____
_____
_____
_____
_____
_____
_____
_____
_____
_____
_____
_____
_____
_____
_____
_____
_____
_____
_____
_____
_____
........Amen
_____

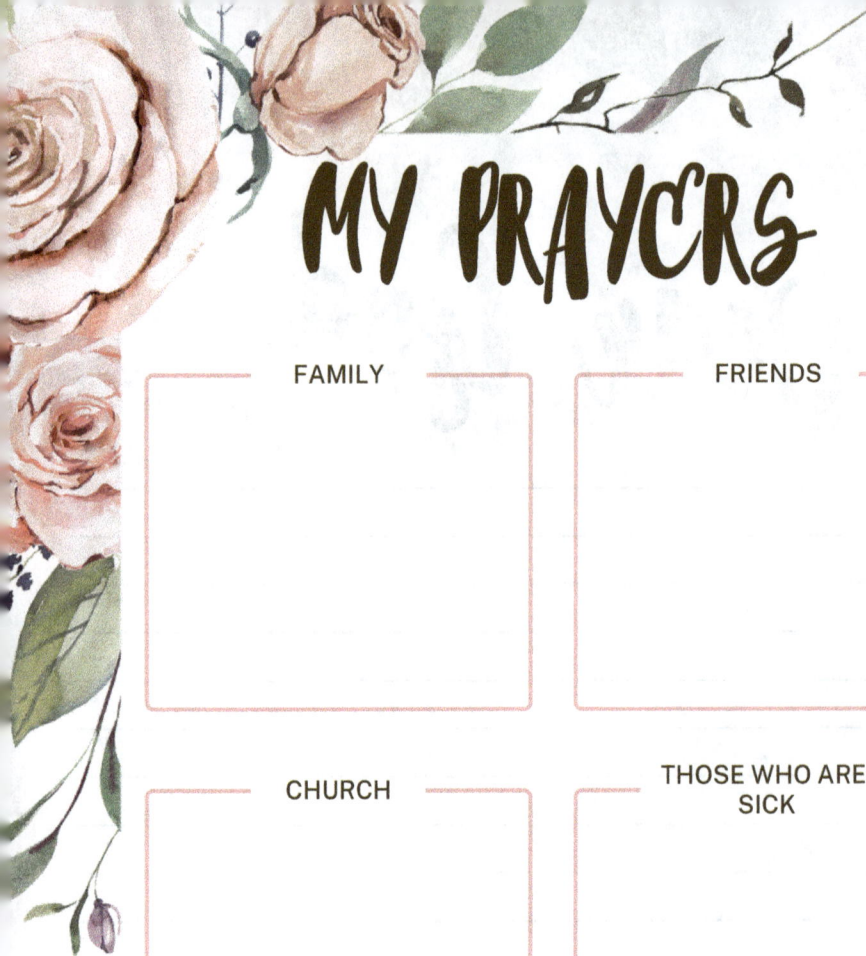

MY PRAYERS

FAMILY

FRIENDS

CHURCH

THOSE WHO ARE SICK

MYSELF

Verse of the DAy:

Gratitude

Reflection

Specific Prayer

I pray for:

_____
_____
_____
_____
_____
_____
_____
_____
_____
_____

Thank You Jesus

Scriptures:

☑   ☑

God, please help me to make peace with yesterday and have an open mind and heart today. Help me to be a blessing. Help me to see You in others and for them to see You in me. Fill me with the Holy Spirit.

In Jesus' Mighty Name, Amen

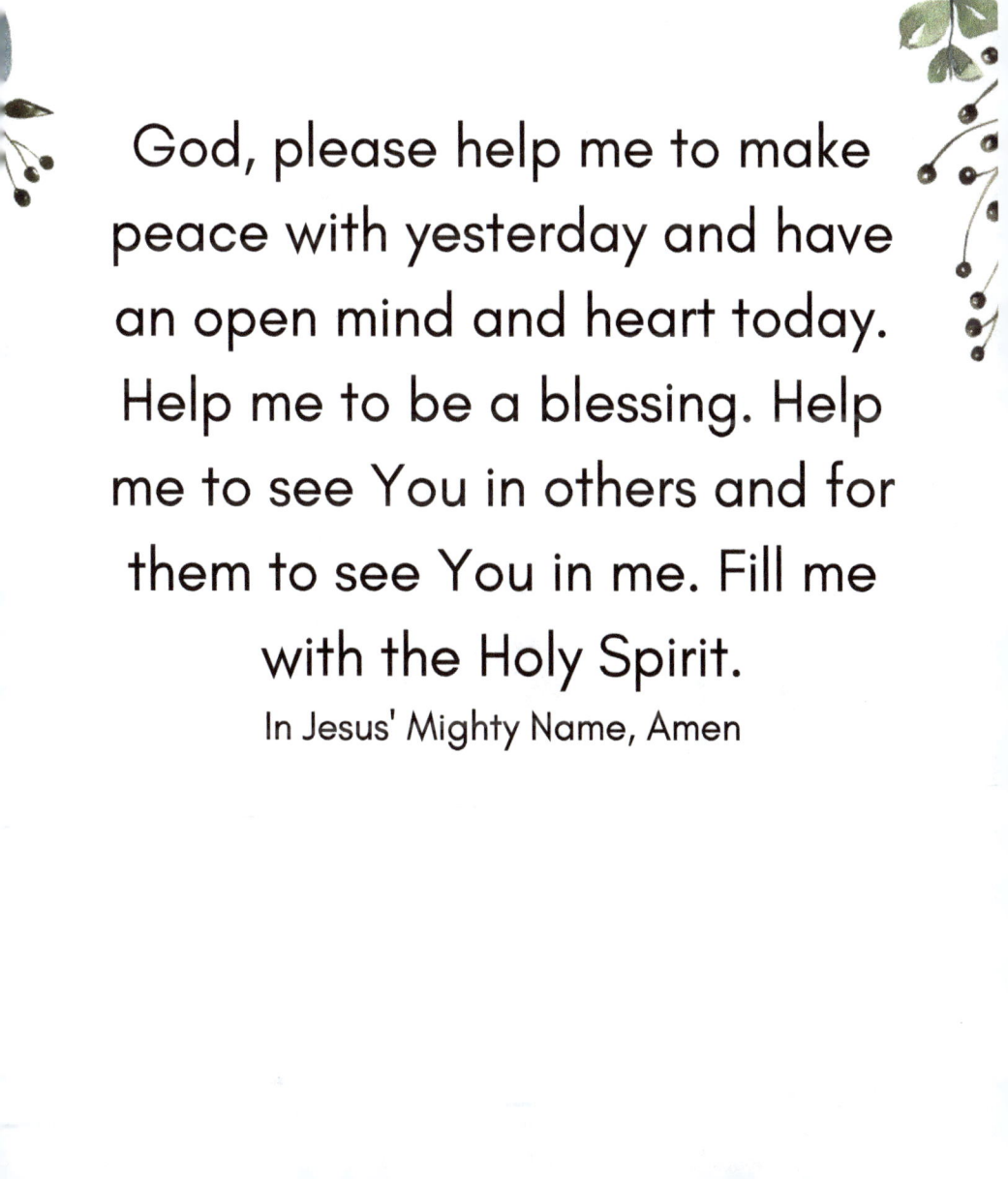

I'm thankful for:

Inspirational Scripture.....

-
-
-
-

Lord help me.....

Reflection

Do not wear yourself out to get rich; do not trust your own cleverness. Cast but a glance at riches, and they are gone, for they will surely sprout wings and fly off to the sky like an eagle.

Proverbs 23:4-5

Prayers

So then, just as you received Christ Jesus as Lord, continue to live your lives in him, rooted and built up in him, strengthened in the faith as you were taught, and overflowing with thankfulness. See to it that no one takes you captive through hollow and deceptive philosophy, which depends on human tradition and the elemental spiritual forces of this world rather than on Christ.

Colossians 2:6–8

Dear God,

_____
_____
_____
_____
_____
_____
_____
_____
_____
_____
_____
_____
_____
_____
_____
_____
_____
_____
_____
_____
_____
_____
.........Amen
_____

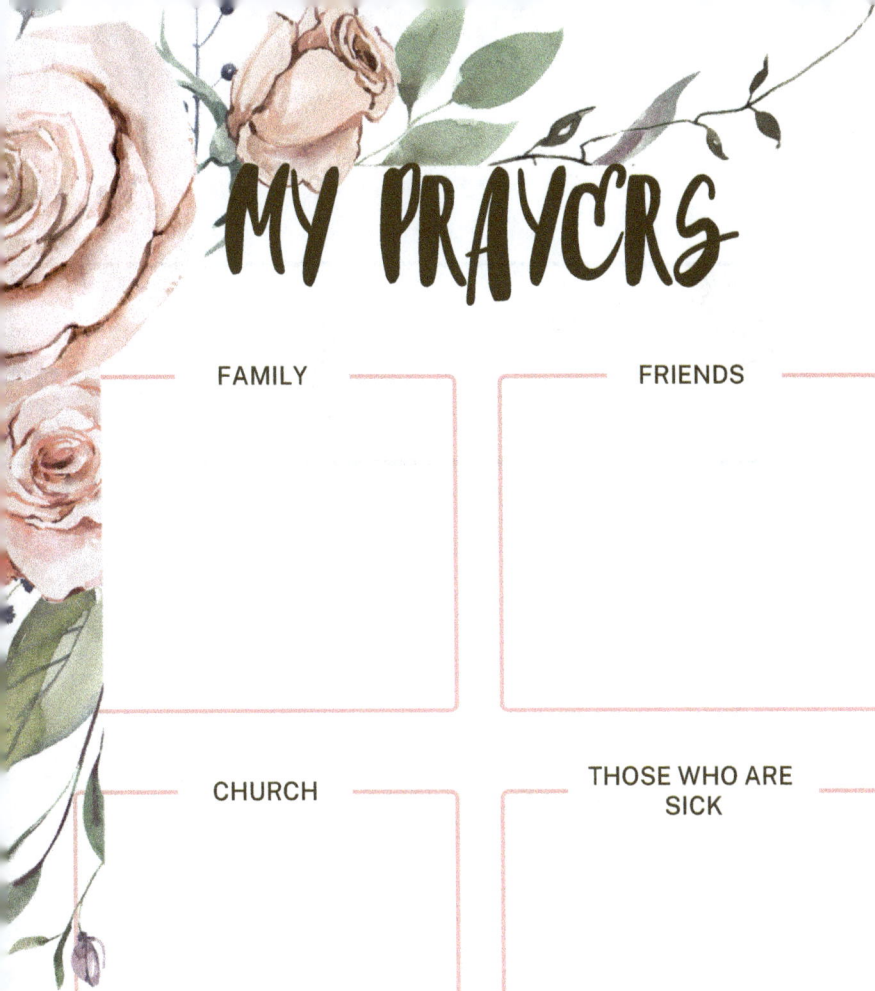

MY PRAYERS

FAMILY

FRIENDS

CHURCH

THOSE WHO ARE SICK

MYSELF

Verse of the Day:

Gratitude

Reflection

Specific Prayer

Thank You Jesus

I pray for:

_____
_____
_____
_____
_____
_____
_____
_____
_____
_____

Scriptures:

☑   ☑

Lord please create in me a clean heart and renew the right spirit within.

In Jesus' Mighty Name, Amen

I'm thankful for:

spirational Scripture.....

Lord help me.....

Reflection

Good judgment wins favor, but the way of the unfaithful leads to their destruction.

Proverbs 13:15

Prayers

A good person leaves an inheritance for their children's children, but a sinner's wealth is stored up for the righteous.

Proverbs 13:22

Dear God,

_____
_____
_____
_____
_____
_____
_____
_____
_____
_____
_____
_____
_____
_____
_____
_____
_____
_____
_____
_____
_____
_____
........Amen
_____
_____

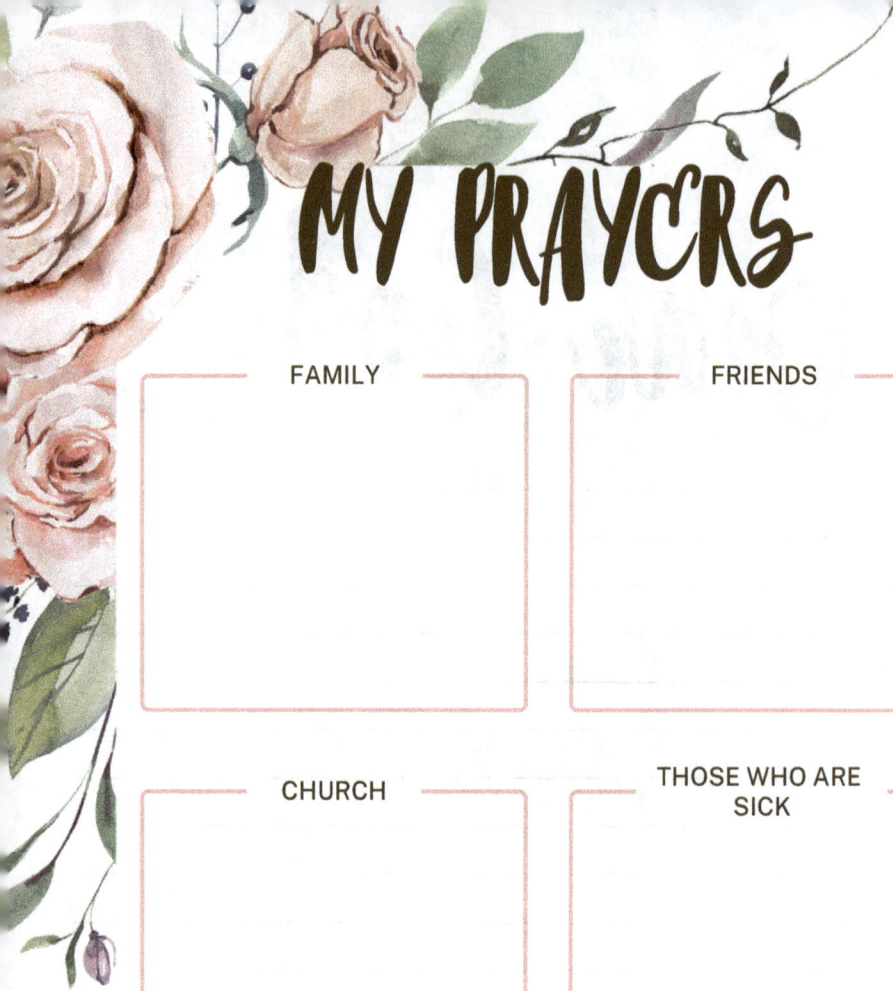

MY PRAYERS

FAMILY

FRIENDS

CHURCH

THOSE WHO ARE SICK

MYSELF

Verse of the Day:

Gratitude

Reflection

Specific Prayer

Thank You Jesus

I pray for:

_____
_____
_____
_____
_____
_____
_____
_____
_____

Scriptures:

☑   ☑

Father God, thank you for
the breath in my lungs and
another day to experience
Your loving kindness!
In Jesus' Mighty Name, Amen

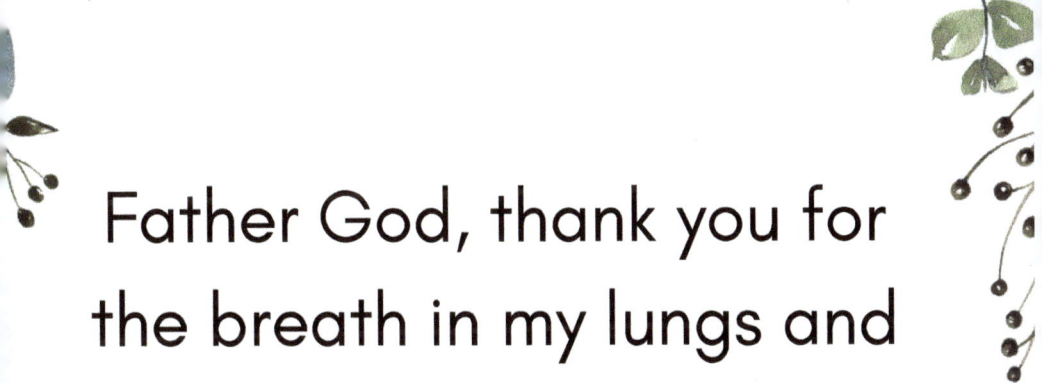

I'm thankful for:

Inspirational Scripture.....

-
-
-
-

Lord help me.....

Reflection

You desire but do not have, so you kill. You covet but you cannot get what you want, so you quarrel and fight. You do not have because you do not ask God.

James 4:2

Prayers

And if we know
that he hears us
whatever we ask
we know that we
have what we
asked of him.

John 15:5

Dear God,

_____
_____
_____
_____
_____
_____
_____
_____
_____
_____
_____
_____
_____
_____
_____
_____
_____
_____
_____
_____
_____
.......Amen

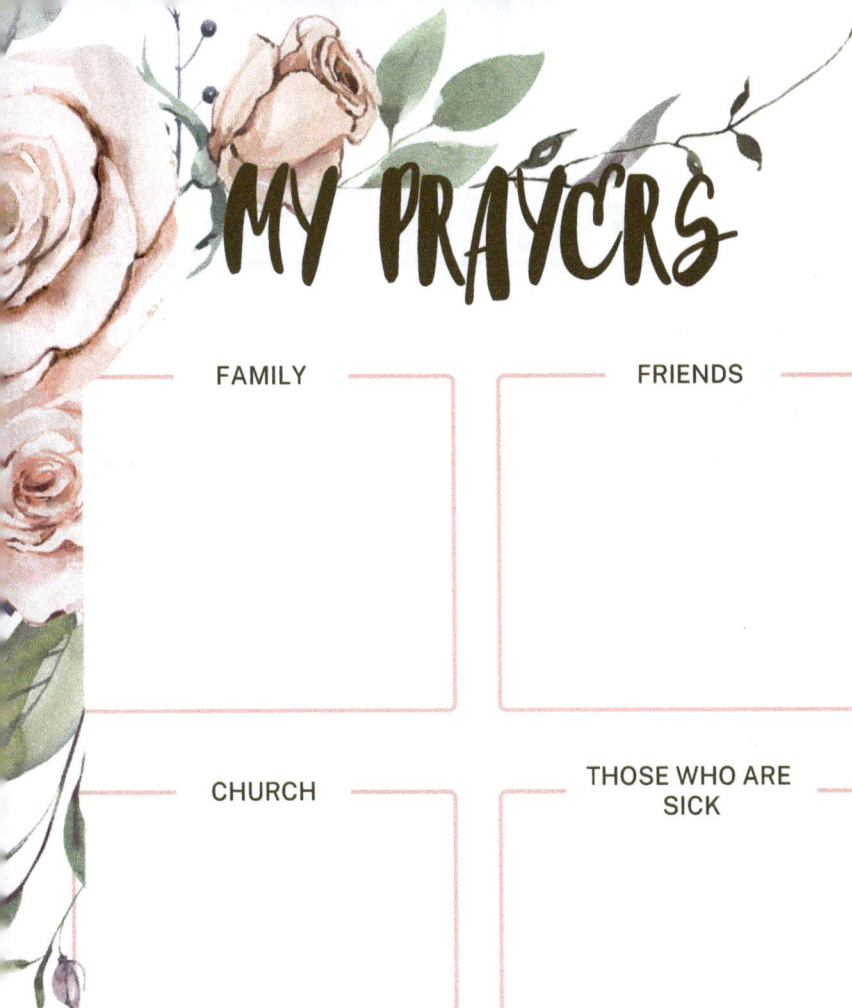

MY PRAYERS

FAMILY

FRIENDS

CHURCH

THOSE WHO ARE SICK

MYSELF

Verse of the Day:

Gratitude

Reflection

Specific Prayer

Thank You Jesus

I pray for:

_____
_____
_____
_____
_____
_____
_____
_____
_____

Scriptures:
☑   ☑

Father please fill me with your grace and mercy, that I may be able to extend the same grace and mercy to others.

In Jesus' Mighty Name, Amen

I'm thankful for:

spirational Scripture.....

Lord help me.....

Reflection

Rejoice always, pray without ceasing, give thanks in all circumstances; for this is the will of God in Christ Jesus for you.

Thessalonians 5:16-18

Prayers

Therefore confess your sins to each other and pray for each other so that you may be healed. The prayer of a righteous person is powerful and effective.

James 5:16

Dear God,

_____
_____
_____
_____
_____
_____
_____
_____
_____
_____
_____
_____
_____
_____
_____
_____
_____
_____
_____
_____
_____
_____
.........Amen
_____

MY PRAYERS

FAMILY

FRIENDS

CHURCH

THOSE WHO ARE SICK

MYSELF

Verse of the DAy:

Gratitude

Reflection

Specific Prayer

I pray for:

_____
_____
_____
_____
_____
_____
_____
_____
_____
_____

Thank You Jesus

Scriptures:

☑   ☑

Lord, DO IT!

In Jesus' Mighty Name, Amen

I'm thankful for:

Inspirational Scripture.....

Lord help me.....

Reflection

Do not be anxious about anything, but in every situation, by prayer and petition, with thanksgiving, present your requests to God.

Philippians 4:6

Prayers

If you, then, though you are evil, know how to give good gifts to your children, how much more will your Father in heaven give good gifts to those who ask him!

Matthew 7:11

Dear God,

_____
_____
_____
_____
_____
_____
_____
_____
_____
_____
_____
_____
_____
_____
_____
_____
_____
_____
_____
_____
_____
_____
.......Amen
_____

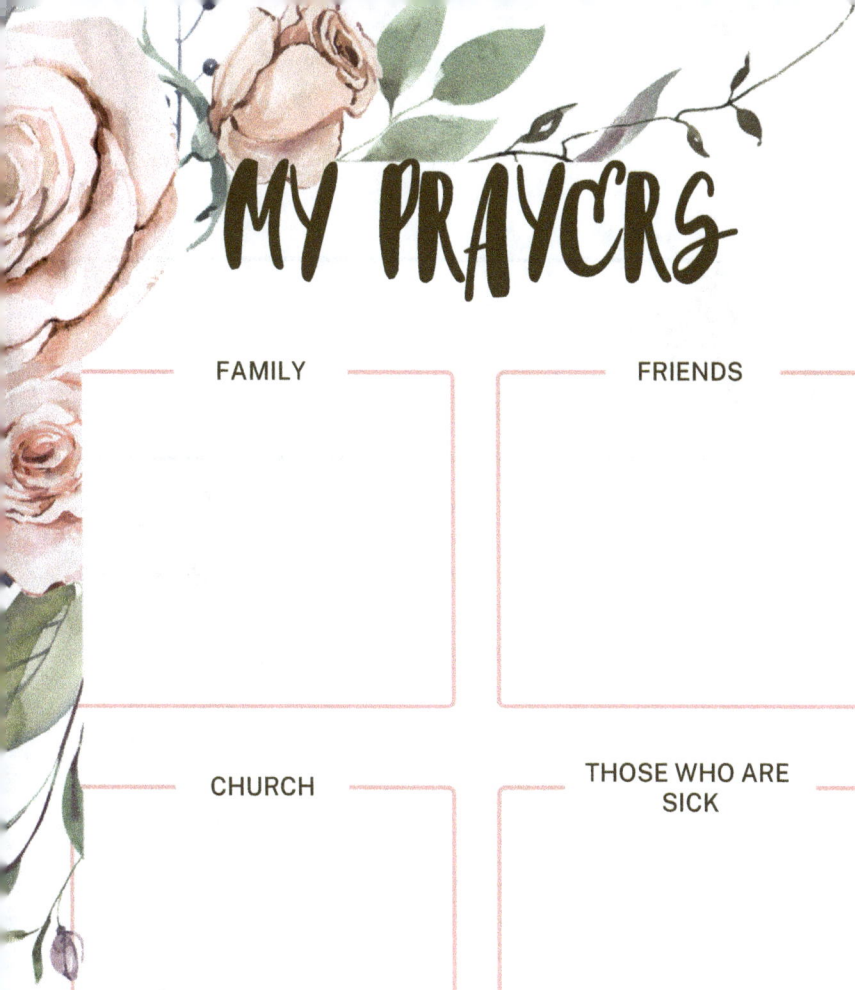

MY PRAYERS

FAMILY

FRIENDS

CHURCH

THOSE WHO ARE SICK

MYSELF

Verse of the DAy:

Gratitude

Reflection

Specific Prayer

I pray for:

_____
_____
_____
_____
_____
_____
_____
_____
_____

Thank You Jesus

Scriptures:
☑   ☑

Lord, I don't come asking for anything. I just want to say Thank You for Everything.

In Jesus' Mighty Name, Amen

I'm thankful for:

Inspirational Scripture.....

Lord help me.....

Reflection

Watch and
pray so that
you will not
fall into
temptation.
The spirit is
willing, but
the flesh is
weak.

Matthew 26:41

Prayers

BIBLE STUDY

DATE	PREACHER	SERMON TOPIC/PASSAGE

NOTES

_____
_____
_____
_____
_____
_____
_____
_____
_____
_____
_____
_____

KEY VERSES

APPLICATION FOR THE WEEK

REFLECTIONS

BIBLC STUDY

NOTES

KEY VERSES

APPLICATION FOR THE WEEK

REFLECTIONS

BIBLC STUDY

DATE	PREACHER	SERMON TOPIC/PASSAGE

NOTES

_____
_____
_____
_____
_____
_____
_____
_____
_____
_____
_____

KEY VERSES

APPLICATION FOR THE WEEK

REFLECTIONS

BIBLE STUDY

DATE	PREACHER	SERMON TOPIC/PASSAGE

NOTES

_____
_____
_____
_____
_____
_____
_____
_____
_____
_____
_____
_____

KEY VERSES

APPLICATION FOR THE WEEK

REFLECTIONS

BIBLE STUDY

DATE	PREACHER	SERMON TOPIC/PASSAGE

NOTES

_____
_____
_____
_____
_____
_____
_____
_____
_____
_____
_____
_____

KEY VERSES

APPLICATION FOR THE WEEK

REFLECTIONS

BIBLC STUDY

DATE	PREACHER	SERMON TOPIC/PASSAGE

NOTES

_____
_____
_____
_____
_____
_____
_____
_____
_____
_____
_____
_____

KEY VERSES

APPLICATION FOR THE WEEK

REFLECTIONS

BIBLE STUDY

DATE	PREACHER	SERMON TOPIC/PASSAGE

NOTES

KEY VERSES

APPLICATION FOR THE WEEK

REFLECTIONS

BIBLC STUDY

DATE	PREACHER	SERMON TOPIC/PASSAGE

NOTES

_____
_____
_____
_____
_____
_____
_____
_____
_____
_____
_____

KEY VERSES

APPLICATION FOR THE WEEK

REFLECTIONS

BIBLE STUDY

DATE	PREACHER	SERMON TOPIC/PASSAGE

NOTES

_____
_____
_____
_____
_____
_____
_____
_____
_____
_____
_____
_____

KEY VERSES

APPLICATION FOR THE WEEK

REFLECTIONS

BIBLE STUDY

DATE	PREACHER	SERMON TOPIC/PASSAGE

NOTES

_____
_____
_____
_____
_____
_____
_____
_____
_____
_____
_____
_____
_____

KEY VERSES

APPLICATION FOR THE WEEK

REFLECTIONS

BIBLE STUDY

DATE	PREACHER	SERMON TOPIC/PASSAGE

NOTES

KEY VERSES

_____
_____
_____
_____
_____
_____
_____
_____
_____
_____
_____

APPLICATION FOR THE WEEK

REFLECTIONS

BIBLE STUDY

DATE	PREACHER	SERMON TOPIC/PASSAGE

NOTES

_____
_____
_____
_____
_____
_____
_____
_____
_____
_____
_____

KEY VERSES

APPLICATION FOR THE WEEK

REFLECTIONS

BIBLE STUDY

DATE	PREACHER	SERMON TOPIC/PASSAGE

NOTES

_____
_____
_____
_____
_____
_____
_____
_____
_____
_____
_____
_____

KEY VERSES

APPLICATION FOR THE WEEK

REFLECTIONS

BIBLC STUDY

DATE	PREACHER	SERMON TOPIC/PASSAGE

NOTES

_____
_____
_____
_____
_____
_____
_____
_____
_____
_____
_____
_____
_____

KEY VERSES

APPLICATION FOR THE WEEK

REFLECTIONS

BIBLE STUDY

DATE	PREACHER	SERMON TOPIC/PASSAGE

NOTES

KEY VERSES

APPLICATION FOR THE WEEK

REFLECTIONS

BIBLE STUDY

DATE	PREACHER	SERMON TOPIC/PASSAGE

NOTES

_____

_____

_____

_____

_____

_____

_____

_____

_____

_____

_____

_____

KEY VERSES

APPLICATION FOR THE WEEK

REFLECTIONS

PRAYER REQUESTS

DATE	NAME	REQUEST

ANSWERED PRAYERS

PRAYER REQUESTS

DATE	NAME	REQUEST

ANSWERED PRAYERS

PRAYER REQUESTS

DATE	NAME	REQUEST

ANSWERED PRAYERS

PRAYER REQUESTS

DATE	NAME	REQUEST

ANSWERED PRAYERS

PRAYER REQUESTS

DATE	NAME	REQUEST

ANSWERED PRAYERS

PRAYER REQUESTS

DATE	NAME	REQUEST

ANSWERED PRAYERS

PRAYER REQUESTS

DATE	NAME	REQUEST

ANSWERED PRAYERS

PRAYER REQUESTS

DATE	NAME	REQUEST

ANSWERED PRAYERS

NOTES

NOTES

NOTES

_____
_____
_____
_____
_____
_____
_____
_____
_____
_____
_____
_____
_____
_____
_____
_____
_____
_____
_____
_____
_____
_____
_____
_____
_____

NOTES

NOTES

NOTES

NOTES

NOTES

NOTES

NOTES

NOTES

www.ingramcontent.com/pod-product-compliance
Lightning Source LLC
Chambersburg PA
CBHW070638150426
42811CB00050B/382